AT YOUR SERVICE

English as a Second Language for Success in Customer Service

KATHLEEN BRADLEY AMIDEI

Archway Publishing books may be ordered through booksellers or by contacting:

Archway Publishing
1663 Liberty Drive
Bloomington, IN 47403
www.archwaypublishing.com
844-669-3957

Because of the dynamic nature of the Internet, any web addresses or links contained in this book may have changed since publication and may no longer be valid. The views expressed in this work are solely those of the author and do not necessarily reflect the views of the publisher, and the publisher hereby disclaims any responsibility for them.

Any people depicted in stock imagery provided by Getty Images are models, and such images are being used for illustrative purposes only.
Certain stock imagery © Getty Images.

ISBN: 978-1-6657-3882-8 (sc)
ISBN: 978-1-6657-3883-5 (e)

Library of Congress Control Number: 2023902600

Print information available on the last page.

Archway Publishing rev. date: 03/10/2023

Dear Students,

Welcome to *"At Your Service-English as a Second Language for Success in Customer Service"*. I have designed this class to equip you with the specialized English necessary to succeed in hospitality, restaurant, retail, and all customer interactions. Using "professional" English effectively will be the key to getting hired and will play a critical role in your ability to help your customers and be promoted throughout your career. I hope you will learn in this class that customer service/hospitality is not just a job, but a rewarding career.

Before we get started, I'd like to tell you a bit about my experience in this field. I started my career with Pan American Airlines as an International Flight Attendant. In my world travels, I learned that using English in a polite and caring manner is appreciated all over the globe. While I was with Pan Am, I had the opportunity to attend New York University to obtain my Master's Degree in Teaching English as a Second Language. I taught ESL at the American Language Institute at NYU and then transitioned to Hotel Management. I held management positions at luxury hotels in New York and San Francisco over a seventeen year period. During that time, I also taught many customer service and ESL classes at the hotels.

After I started teaching at the College of Marin in 2009, I noticed that many students worked in hotels, stores, restaurants, and health care. I realized that I could help them succeed by combining my knowledge of teaching ESL with my hospitality background. I have created this class especially for you. In the years I have been teaching it, my students have gotten jobs and been promoted. They have told me that this class has been invaluable for them.

I hope it helps you, too!!!

Kathleen Bradley Amidei

At Your Service
English as a Second Language for Customer Service

By Kathleen Bradley Amidei

Table of Contents

- *Encourage employee input/solicit ideas.*
- *Think like a manager/owner*
- *Offer to learn new areas/positions.*
- *Offer to help new employees.*
- *Arrive early/stay late/ Offer to work overtime.*
- *Suggest improvements for workplace procedures.*

- *Customer-focused employees create a positive bottom line.*
- *How the theory of "Supply and Demand" impacts pricing.*

- *Serving Wine and beverages. Improve your wine IQ.*
- *Taking food orders.*
- *Experience at a casual restaurant.*

Unit 1

SUPERCHARGE YOUR PROFESSIONAL ENGLISH

Let's use this class to think about the following concepts of good service:
(We will concentrate on all of these throughout the semester.)

1.) *Increase your awareness quotient.*

2.) *Anticipate customer needs and wants.*

3.) *Ensure the customer feels special.*

4.) *Offer a choice (whenever possible).*

5.) *Personalize your service.*

6.) *Train well/know your job ...and more.*

7.) *Help your customer with everything you can; not just what is in your job description.*

8.) *Initiate engagement with the five E's: eye contact, ear-to-ear smile, enthusiastic greeting, engage, educate to make a positive connection.*

Which concept will you concentrate on this semester?

(Example): I plan to focus on number four- I'd like to offer my customer a choice whenever I can.

Professional English
Why?

Let's start our class with a question. Why is language so important when talking to our customers? Why bother trying to improve yours? Why does it matter?

1.) Think of a time, recently, when you were a customer and someone gave you great service. What did that look like? How did you feel?

- Language- Do you remember any specific words or phrases?

  _____

  _____

  _____

- Actions/Body Language – what did that look like?

  _____

  _____

  _____

- How did you feel? Would you return? Would you tell your friends? Would you write about it on a website?

  _____

  _____

  _____

2.) Think of a time when you received inattentive, rude, or uncaring service? What did it look like? How did you feel?

- Language- Do you remember any specific words or phrases?

  _____

  _____

  _____

- Actions/Body Language-what did that look like?

  _____

  _____

  _____

How did you feel? Would you return? Would you tell your friends? Would you write about it on a website?

Everything "Communicates"
(Does everything have to use spoken language to communicate?)

1.) What does this mean to you?

_____

_____

What does the picture above communicate to you?

_____

Let's make a list of everything in our classroom:

1.) *carpet* _____

2.) _____

3.) _____

4.) _____

5.) _____

6.) _____

7.) _____

8.) _____

Activity: "Everything Communicates"

Directions:

This is an opportunity to test your ability to observe your surroundings. Within the next week, please go to a bank, retail store (for example: Macy's, CVS, Walgreens), super market, or restaurant. Observe the interactions of the people who work there. Make a list of everything you see and hear. Please be prepared to present your findings to the class.

What did you see?

1. Floor- is it clean?
2. _____
3. _____
4. _____
5. _____
6. _____
7. _____
8. _____
9. _____
10. _____

What did you hear? Polite and friendly or discourteous interactions?

_____
_____
_____
_____
_____

Unit 2

BODY LANGUAGE

Body Language

How do we express ourselves without saying a word to our customers?

1.) **Eyes: good eye contact shows that you are interested in your customers.**

2.) **Active Listening:**
- **don't interrupt.**
- **nodding head slightly in agreement shows that you care.**

3.) Hands and arms:

- not crossed but should be open.
- open arms show that you are receptive to your customers.

4.) Good Posture:

- shows energy, confidence, and professionalism.

5.) Facial Expression:

- Welcoming smile.

Would you like to improve your body language? Which area would you like to focus on this semester?

How About That Body Language!!

> (Nancy is a server in a local restaurant in Marin County. She has just served her customer a hamburger. He motions to her to come over to his table.)

Nancy: Did you want something else? _(As she is talking to him, she is looking down at the floor.)_

Mr. Jones: Oh, yes, I just wanted to tell you…….

Nancy: _(She's in a hurry and interrupts him.)_ Oh, I know. The chef has been making mistakes all day and he over cooked your burger.

Mr. Jones: Well, no. If you would let me finish my sentence I was going to tell you how good this hamburger is!!

Nancy: Well, that's a surprise!! _(Her arms are folded and her posture is terrible!!)_

Is This Better Body Langauge?

> **(Nancy Just Served A Hamburger To Her Customer A Few Minutes Ago.)**

Nancy: How is everything? *(She makes good eye contact with her customer.)*

Mr. Jones: This is delicious!! Oh, could I have a little more dressing for my salad?

Nancy: Oh, certainly. I'll get that right away. *(Her arms are open and she has good posture.)* I'll tell the chef how much you liked your burger!

Unit 3
CONNECTING WITH YOUR CUSTOMERS

***Section A* -In this unit we will examine our approach
to ensuring our customers feel SPECIAL.**

"To give real service you must add something which cannot be bought or measured with money, and that is sincerity and integrity."
Douglas Adams, author

Our customers want to feel well-treated. That is a basic unspoken need of every human. This unit focuses on the idea that if you have your customer in front of you (or on the phone or on a website), why not use the time well. Use it as an opportunity, not only to give basic service, but to also make them feel special. When we use the best language to connect or engage with our customers, we can ensure we are customizing our service for each customer and help our business.

At the end of this unit you will:
- *Know the difference between a basic transaction and positively interacting with your customers.*
- *Know how to use the correct language to make a positive connection with your customers.*

1. *Think about these concepts:*

   - *Treat every customer as if he/she is important.*
   - *Focus on each customer as an individual.*
   - *Treat your customers the way they would like to be treated.*
   - *Engage and connect. What does this mean to you?*
   - *Listen and respond in a personalized manner.*

Your Opinion

Let's listen to a variety of customer situations:

Scenario One: Mrs. Jones would like to return an item at a department store. Mrs. Jones has been waiting in line.

Mary (salesclerk) - Can I help you?

Mrs. Jones- Yes, I'd like to return this. I received it for Christmas and it's too small.

Mary- OK, I'll process a gift card for you.

Mrs. Jones- Thank you. I'll use it before I go on vacation next month.

Mary- Please sign here and you'll be all set. Here is your gift card and thank you for shopping with us.

Mrs. Jones- Thank you.

Scenario Two: Mrs. Jones would like to return an item at a department store. Mrs. Jones has been waiting in line on a very busy Saturday.

Susan (Salesclerk) - Thank you for waiting. Our sale is very popular today! How may I help you?

Mrs. Jones- Well, I received this for Christmas, but it doesn't fit. May I return it?

Susan- Oh, yes, I'd be happy to help you. Would you like to try it in another size? I can show you several sizes, if you'd like.

Mrs. Jones- Not today. Maybe I'll look another day.

Susan- That's fine. I'll get a gift card processed for you to use anytime you'd like.

Mrs. Jones- That will be great. I'm taking a vacation next month, so maybe I'll come in before I go.

Susan- A vacation?! Great! Let me get this gift card started. And what is your name?

Mrs. Jones- Helen Jones.

Susan- Here is your gift card, Mrs. Jones. And may I ask where you are going on your trip?

Mrs. Jones- Oh, sure. Mexico City. I've never been and have always wanted to go.

Susan – Oh, wonderful! I'm from there!! You will love it!

Mrs. Jones- I've heard great things about it. Any recommendations?

Susan- Oh, Mrs. Jones, there's so much to do there. Definitely see the famous museum and gorgeous Chapultepec Park.

Mrs. Jones-Thank you so much! You have been so helpful! I'll come in to shop before I go.

Susan- I look forward to helping you!

Discuss the differences between scenario one and two with your partner. What did Mary do?
_Scenario one _____

_____

_____

_____

_____

What did Susan do ? _Scenario two

_____

_____

_____

_____

_____

Let's listen to Miriam as she greets her guests at a local hotel in Marin County.)

Miriam: Welcome to the Marin Vista Hotel. We are happy to have you as our guests. What is your name?

Mr. Diaz: Diaz. Juan Diaz. We are happy to be here.

Miriam: Oh, is this your first time in our area, Mr. Diaz?
OR
What brings you to our area?
OR
Are you here for a special event? *(if you see a wedding gown)*

Mr. Diaz: Yes. We are here to attend the County Fair. We'd like to find out about some other things to do in the area.

Miriam: Oh, you are really going to enjoy that! Your children will have a great time!! They have lots of rides and farm animals. I can help you with some other activities in the area. Let me get you checked in to your room and then I can help you.

Mr. Diaz: Thanks very much. That would be great!

(After she checks them in, she helps them have a great vacation!! What are some of the special things she can recommend? What can she do to make them feel special?)

Section B. How do we connect/engage with our customers? What language and opportunities are important?

MATCH the following with the best way to engage/connect with your customer.

If your customer says:

    A. "This is our first time here." __**3**____
    B. " I'm going on vacation."_____
    C. " I just moved here."_____
    D. "We are not familiar with your area."_____
    E. " I'm going to a special party."_____
    F. " I just got a new job." _____

1. I'd be happy to help you find the perfect dress. What kind of party is it?
2. Congratulations! Time to celebrate! What can I get you? Will you be working in this area?
3. Oh, great. I love to help new customers. Let me explain our menu in a little more detail. Where are you from?
4. Can I help you with directions or maybe some restaurant recommendations?
5. This shirt will be perfect for a vacation. May I ask where you are going?
6. Where did you move from? Our weather here is great!

Section C. Practice connecting or engaging with your "customers" (your partner in class,)

1. Is this your first time in our restaurant?
2. Is this your first time in our area?
3. What brings you to our area/restaurant/store?
4. Did you see the Super Bowl last night/ Great game!
5. Those Warriors are something else! Aren't they?
6. Weather: Isn't this a beautiful day?

7. I hope it warms up soon.

8. I've never seen so much rain!

9. It looks like you are here for a special occasion.

Section D: Brainstorming Ideas

Collaborate in groups of four with your suggestions for connecting/engaging with your customers.

1. _____

2. _____

3. _____

4. _____

5. _____

Homework: Unit 2

Connecting/engaging with your customers

Try this experiment at a store, bank, or anywhere you are a customer:

As a customer, mention one of our "**connection phrases**" to the person who is helping you in the store, bank, gas station, restaurant, or hotel.

Examples:
"Nice weather today"
"I've never been here before."
"I really like this _____ (restaurant, store, etc.)"
"I need this _____ (dress, shirt, etc) for my cousin's wedding."

Does the person in the store respond to you in an engaged, personalized way? Do they ignore what you have said and just go through the basic motions of completing the transaction? Please write your experiences below and be prepared to tell the class about them.

Experience 1

_____

_____

_____

_____

_____

Experience 2

_____

_____

_____

_____

_____

Unit 4

GRACIOUS AND PROFESSIONAL LANGUAGE

Gracious Language

Using the most courteous and amiable English to help our guests

---

This unit will focus on the very most polite, courteous, professional, and gracious language to use with our guests. It is important to note that casual language has a place in our lives (possibly with friends or family), but it is important to know when to use casual language and when to use gracious, professional language. The following is a partial list of some of the most useful examples of gracious language to replace the more casual (or in some examples, incorrect) English .Sometimes, we are trying to be polite, but, because we don't know the gracious language, it sounds almost rude or too abrupt.

Casual Language	Gracious Language
1. Are you done?	1. Are you finished? May I take your plate?
2. Yeah.	2. Yes.
3. Sure, no problem. Hey, no problem.	3. Certainly, I am happy to do that for you. You're welcome.
4. What do you guys want? Do you know what you want?	4. Have you decided what you would like? Have you made a selection?
5. I can do that.	5. I will be happy to do that for you. I will be happy to get that for you. It would be my pleasure.
6. Can I help you?	6. May I help you? May I assist you?
Do you want_____? How about some___? You want wine?	May I offer you some warm bread? Would you like to see that sweater in another color? May I suggest our special of the day? It's very popular. May I show you our newest model? May I recommend the steak?

Casual Language	**Gracious Language**
7. Lady, sit here. (This is never correct English.)	7. Ma'am, would you like to sit here? Miss, would you like to sit here?
8. I don't know.	8. I am not sure, but let me find out about that immediately for you. I will just take a minute.
9. We are all out of that. We don't have that.	9. I am so sorry, but we are out of your selection. May I offer you_____?
10. No.	10. I am terribly sorry but we can't do that at the moment. Let me offer you an alternative.
11. Wait here.	11. Would you mind waiting just a few minutes? We'll have that ready for you very shortly.
12. It's over there. (pointing)	12. Allow me to show you the way. Let me escort you.
13. Give me a minute.	13. If you could just give me a minute, I'll be happy to help you.

Let's practice some of our new gracious phrases with a partner.

Gracious Language

SCENARIO ONE
(The guest looks like they have finished their meal. Always wait until everyone at the table looks like they have finished their meals. Do not remove one guest's plate while others at the table are still eating.)

"Are you finished?"
OR
"Are you finished? May I take your plate?"
OR
"Are you still working on that?"

SCENARIO TWO
(The guest asks you for something.)
"May we have more bread?"
"May we have some olive oil?"

Your response should be:

"Certainly, I am happy to get that for you."

SCENARIO THREE
(You have just given the guest more bread and they thank you.)

Your response should be:

"You're welcome."

SCENARIO FOUR
(You show the guest to the table.)

"Ma'm, would you like to sit here?"
"Miss, would you like to sit here?"

SCENARIO FIVE
(You have given the guests their menus and have given them some time to look at the menu.)

"Have you decided what you would like?"
OR
"Have you made a selection?"

SCENARIO SIX
(You are offering the menu to the guest)
"May I offer you our menu?"
"Would you like our menu?"
"May I show you our wine list?"
(The guest asks for your suggestions. They want some advice.)
"May I suggest the halibut/"
"May I recommend the steak? It's very popular."

SCENARIO SEVEN
(The guest asks for something.)
"I'll be happy to do that for you."
"I'll be happy to get that for you."
"It would be my pleasure."

SCENARIO EIGHT
(Anytime you want to offer help.)
"May I help you?"
"May I assist you?"

SCENARIO NINE
(The guest asks you a question but you don't know the answer.)
"I am not sure, but let me find out immediately for you. I will just take a minute."

SCENARIO TEN
(The guest orders Halibut but the chef has just told you that he doesn't have any left tonight.)
"I am so sorry but we are out of your selection. May I offer you the tuna? It's very good also."

SCENARIO ELEVEN
(The guest has just checked in to the hotel at 10:30pm and wants to eat in the restaurant, but it is closed.)

"I'm so sorry but our restaurant closes at 10pm. We have a great Room Service menu with many of the same dishes. I will be happy to expedite your order for you."

SCENARIO TWELVE
(The guest's table needs to be set up.)

"Would you mind waiting just a few minutes? We'll have that ready for you very shortly."

SCENARIO THIRTEEN
(The guest asks you for directions.)

"Allow me to show you the way."

"Let me escort you."

Let's take a look at the importance of using gracious language in a restaurant.

Would you like to eat in this restaurant?

Mr. and Mrs. Jones are celebrating their fifth wedding anniversary and have been looking forward to going to **The Steakhouse Restaurant** *for several weeks. Mr. Jones told the person who took the reservation that it was their anniversary. They have never eaten there, but they have heard that the food is good.*

Greeter (Maitre'd)- Hi, Guys. You want some food? *(He looks at the floor)*

Mr. Jones- Yes. We have a reservation. The name is Phil Jones.

Greeeter- Hey, no problem. Lady, sit here.

Mr. Jones- We'd like to sit at that table near the window.

Greeter- Oh, no. We can't seat anyone there. We aren't using that part of the restaurant tonight.

Waiter- What do you guys want?

Mr. Jones- What comes with the steak?

Waiter- It's right there on the menu. Can't you see? Vegetables and potatoes.

Mr. Jones- Oh, I didn't see that. Can I have French fries with my steak?

Waiter- Oh, no. We don't do special substitutions. The Chef doesn't like it.

Mr. Jones- Well, we'd like to order some wine first.

Waiter- Oh, ok. What do you guys want?

Mr. Jones- We'd like the Rodney Strong Cabernet Sauvignon.

Waiter- Oh, we don't have that one. All out.

Mr. Jones- Well, how about the Merlot?

Waiter- Yah, We have it. OK. And what do you want to eat, lady?

Mrs. Jones- I'd like the prime rib medium rare, please.

Waiter- O.K. It usually comes out medium. Just letting you know. Don't blame me.

Mr. and Mrs. Jones are served their meal. Then, about 20 minutes later...............

Waiter- Are you done?

Mrs. Jones- No, I'm still eating. Could I have some more au jus and horse radish?

Waiter- No, we're all out of that.

A little later......

Waiter- What do you guys want for dessert?

Mr. Jones- We'll have the crème brulee with two spoons.

Waiter- Hmmm......let's see....oh, yeah, we don't have that tonight. Don't blame me.

What did you notice about the language used at the Steakhouse Restaurant?

Directions: Please underline the gracious language used with the customers at the Park Grill restaurant in the next skit.

Would you like to eat in this restaurant?

*Mr. and Mrs. Sanchez are celebrating Mrs. Sanchez's 38th birthday. They have been looking forward to dining at the **Park Grill** for several weeks. When Mr. Sanchez made the reservation, the **Park Grill** reservation agent asked if they were celebrating anything special and he told them it was his wife's birthday. They have never eaten there but they have heard the food is very good.*

Greeter (Maitre'd) - Welcome to the Park Grill. **<u>We are delighted</u>** to have you as our guests. Do you have a reservation? *(good eye contact)*

Mr. Sanchez- Yes. My name is Sanchez. Enrique Sanchez. We are happy to be here, also.

Greeter- Very good, Mr. and Mrs. Sanchez. We have a special table all prepared for you. Would you like to sit near the window or **would you prefer** the banquette on the side?

Mr. Sanchez- What would you like, honey?

Mrs. Sanchez- Oh, I'd prefer the window table.

Greeter- Very good, Mr. and Mrs. Sanchez. Allow me to show you to your table.

He escorts them to their table.

Greeter- I hope you like this table. Mrs. Sanchez, we would like to wish you a very happy birthday. Thank you so much for choosing the Park Grill for your special occasion. If there is anything I can help you with, please do not hesitate to ask. Our chef has some wonderful specials this evening. And may I introduce your server, Michelle? She will take very good care of you tonight.

Mr. and Mrs. Sanchez- Thank you very much.

Server- Welcome, again, to the Park Grill. May I offer you bottled water or regular water?

Mr. Sanchez- Oh, regular will be fine.

Server- May I show you our wine list or would you like a cocktail before dinner?

Mr. Sanchez- Yes, we'd like the wine list, please. We'll have wine with dinner.

Server- Mr. and Mrs. Sanchez, may I tell you about our specials? Our chef has been outdoing himself in the kitchen. Tonight we are offering a fresh Alaskan halibut on a bed of spicy lentils, rack of lamb with a Dijon hazelnut crust and our pasta special is fettuccine alle vongole. I'll give you some time to think about all this and be right back with some of our special warm bread and butter.

A bit later.........

Server- Have you decided what you would like?

Mr. Sanchez- Yes, my wife would like the halibut and I'll have the rack of lamb. Is it possible to have the lentils with my lamb?

Server- Oh, certainly. **We** are always happy to **customize** anything for you. And how would you like that cooked?

Mr. Sanchez- Medium for both.

Server- And have you made your wine selection, Mr. Sanchez?

Mr. Sanchez- Yes. We'd like the Robert Mondavi Cabernet.

The server brings their entrees and shortly after they are served ....

Server- How is everything? May I get you anything else?

Mr. and Mrs. Sanchez- Everything is wonderful. Thank you.

When it looks like they have finished their meal..........

Server- Are you finished? May I take your plate?

Mr. and Mrs. Sanchez- Yes, That was delicious.

Server- Wonderful. I am so glad you enjoyed everything. May I offer you coffee or dessert?

Mr. Sanchez- Yes. I think we should have a nice dessert.

Server- Here is our dessert menu. May I recommend the chocolate ganache cake? It is very popular.

Mr. Sanchez- That sounds great! Let's have one piece with two spoons.

Server- I will be very happy to get that for you.

The entire wait staff assembles at the Sanchez's table to sing "Happy Birthday" as the server brings the cake with a lit candle on it.

The Sanchezes thanked them very much for the wonderful evening!!!

(The server brings the check and gently places it on the table saying "no rush and thank you again.")

Unit 5:

THE PSYCHOLOGY OF DELIVERING WHAT YOUR CUSTOMER WANTS

In this unit we are going to participate in role-playing and other activities focusing on the best language to achieve the following goals with each customer experience:

- **a**.) Ensure our customers feel **special.**
- **b**.) **Anticipate** our customer's needs.
- **c.)** Offer a **choice** (when possible).
- **d.)** **Tell** our customer what we are going to do **for** them and/or let them know that they will be taken care of shortly.

Why do we want to do this? What is the thinking (psychology) behind these goals? Please write your answer here:

_____

_____

_____

_____

_____

We will also incorporate a review of our **gracious language** from Unit 4.

As we are reading our skits, think about the goals listed above (a,b,c or d).

ACTIVITY ONE: **Scene: Mary is a Front Office Agent at a busy hotel in Marin County. Let's watch as she helps a guest.**

Mary: Welcome to the Marin Garden Hotel. We are happy to have you.

Mr. Jones: Thank you. I am happy to be here, too.

Mary: May I have your name?

Mr. Jones: Yes, Sam Jones.

Mary: Wonderful, Mr. Jones. I see we have your reservation with us for two nights in a deluxe category room. Oh, you are really going to like that. May I offer a choice of a garden view or a pool view? Both are popular.

Mr. Jones: Oh, how nice. I'd prefer the pool view. Even though I'm here for the Computer Convention, I'd still like to relax a little!

Mary: Very good. And I see we have your credit information, so if I could see your identification, we'll be all set. Oh, I'm sure you'll enjoy the convention, but if you would like help with any of the activities in the area, I'd be happy to help you. We also have a great spa here on the property that you might enjoy.

Mr. Jones: Oh, that would be great!
(Mr. Jones starts searching for his cellphone in his pockets.)
Oh, my, I think I left my cellphone in the taxi!! Oh, this is terrible!! And now, I have to run to a meeting here in the hotel!

Mary: Oh, I saw you when you arrived. I know that taxi company, Green Taxi of Marin. Here's what I'll do: I'll call them right away to get in touch with the driver. If the phone is still there, he can bring it to the hotel. I'll take care of everything for you. I'll send a message to you in your meeting room, if you don't mind.

Mr. Jones: Oh, that would be great. I can't miss this meeting, but I also can't live without my phone! *(Mr. Jones runs off to his meeting)*

(Mary quickly calls the taxi company, they contact the driver and he returns to the hotel to deliver Mr. Jones' phone.)

And then after Mr. Jones' meeting...........................

Mr. Jones: You were a life-saver, Mary! You responded so quickly! Thank you so very much for your quick action. I would be lost without my phone; especially on a business trip.

Mary: Mr. Jones, it was my pleasure. I am so happy it all turned out OK!

DISCUSS: *Please discuss the situation above with your partners, focusing on points a,b,c,and d.*

a.) ***Making the guest feel special:*** _____

_____

_____

b.) ***Anticipating the customer's needs:***_____

_____

_____

c.) ***Offering a choice:***_____

_____

_____

d.) ***Informing the customer (Telling the customer what is going on or what you are going to do)***_____

_____

_____

Scene: It is a busy day at Macy's department store. Susan is the salesclerk and enjoys providing exceptional customer service. She always goes out of her way to please her customers. She knows the value of giving her customers the best experience.

There is a big sale at Macy's and customers have to wait in line longer than usual. Susan has to leave the cashier area to check on a price for Mrs. Jones, the customer in front of her. She excuses herself and ALSO informs the next person in line that she will be right back to help them.

Susan: *(Speaking to the next person in line.)*
I'm so sorry you have to wait. I'll be with you in just a quick minute. I have to run and check on this price for this customer and I'll be right back. It will just take a minute. Thank you so much.

(Susan finishes with Mrs. Jones and starts to help Nancy Smith.)

Susan: Thank you again so very much! Did you find everything you were looking for? Will this be all?

Customer/ Nancy Smith: Yes, I found exactly what I was looking for. I also want to thank you for telling me what you were doing. Sometimes sales clerks leave an area and you don't know when they are coming back!!

Susan: Yes, I understand that. I'll process this and you'll be all set. Oh, it looks like you have been successful today!!

(Susan notices a lot of packages and it looks like Mrs. Smith is having a hard time holding on to everything she has bought today.)

Let me help you with your packages. Why don't I put several of them in a larger bag, so it will be easier for you to carry?

Nancy Smith: Oh, that is so kind of you. I really appreciate that. I guess I'm enjoying your sale today!!

Susan: We can also help you carry your packages out to your car, if you'd like.

Nancy Smith: Oh, that won't be necessary, but thank you so much for the offer.

Susan: Certainly. And here you are. All set. Thank you so much for shopping with us today!

Nancy Smith: It was worth the wait! You have been so helpful.

Susan: We look forward to seeing you next time, Mrs. Smith.

DISCUSS: *Please discuss the situation above with your partners. What was the gracious language used? Did Susan achieve the goals of a,b,c or d?*

a.) *Making the guest feel special:*_____

_____

_____

b.) *Anticipating the customer's needs:*_____

_____

_____

c.) *Offering a choice:*_____

_____

_____

d.) *Informing the customer (Telling the customer what is going on)*_____

_____

_____

ACTIVITY 3: Scene: Joe is a server in a busy Marin restaurant. His day got off to a bad start when his car wouldn't start and he had to take the bus to work. He arrived late for his shift and his manager was not pleased. Now he's waiting on his first customer of the day.

Joe: What would you like to order?

Customer/ Ellen: Do you have any specials that are not listed on the menu?

Joe: Oh, yea, I forgot to tell you about them. Let's see....um..oh, yea, we have fish with a sauce and a special steak.

Ellen: Oh, ok. I guess I'll have a salad with extra avocado.

Joe: Anything extra will cost you more. Just sayin'.

Ellen: Oh, that's fine. What dressings do you have?

Joe: The usual.

Ellen: I'd like ranch please.

Joe: We don't have that.

Ellen: OK, then, please bring me oil and vinegar.

Joe: Yea, ok.

30

(Joe leaves the area and does not return to Ellen's table for over twenty minutes.)

Joe: Here you are.

Ellen: Why did this take so long? I have been waiting a long time for just a simple salad.

Joe: Oh, we had a lot of people call in sick and things are slow today.

Ellen: Well, it would have been helpful if you could have told me this would take a long time. Could I have it "to-go" now, because I don't have time to eat it here. I have to get to my class at College of Marin.

Joe: Oh, yea. Here's a box.

DISCUSS: *How was Joe's customer service "score"? What would you have done differently?*

3.) *Making the guest feel special:*_____

_____

_____

4.) *Anticipating the customer's needs:*_____

_____

_____

5.) *Offering a choice:*_____

_____

_____

6.) *Informing the customer (Telling the customer what is going on or what you are going to do)*_____

_____

_____

ACTIVITY FOUR: Think about your current job or a job you would like to have in the future. Tell your partner some of the ways you can start using the concepts of a, b, c, and d above. Make a list of your suggestions and report these to the class:

_____

_____

_____

_____

_____

_____

Unit 6

GIVING DIRECTIONS

It is always helpful to be able to give accurate and precise directions to our guests. The use of prepositions in English can be a bit confusing. Let's look at some good examples.

Helpful Words for Directions

Prepositions

next to
through
across from
beside
opposite
on the left/right
straight ahead
by
down the hall
beyond
past

Verbs

Escort
take
Show
turn left/right

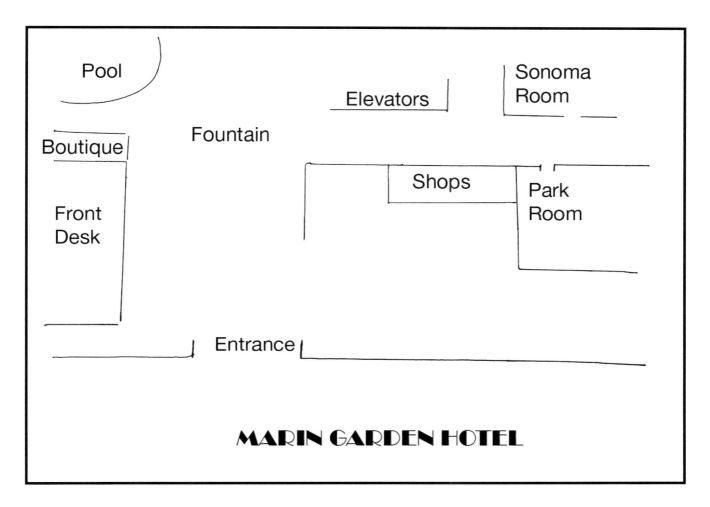

Jane is the door person at <u>the **Marin** Garden Hotel</u>. She greets guests with a smile and is often the first worker whom the guests meet at the hotel. Please look at the map of the Marin Garden Hotel on page .

Visitor: Excuse me. Can you tell me where the Park Room is? I have a meeting there.

Jane: Certainly. I'd be happy to help you with that, Ma'am. You **should** go through the lobby. Then, turn right at the elevators and continue past the shops. **You will see** the Park Room on your right, just opposite the Sonoma Room. Enjoy your meeting!

Visitor: Thank you so much!

A few minutes later.....

Guest: I forgot my cellphone charger. Do you have any in the hotel?

Jane: Oh, yes, Sir. We have every type of charger. **Let me escort you** to the front desk and they will be able to help you with that.

The Jones family approaches Jane with a question.....

Mrs. Jones: It's such a nice day! We'd like to go swimming, but we can't find the pool! Can you help us?

Jane: We have a beautiful pool. I know you'll enjoy it! **You should go** straight ahead and **you'll see** a fountain. Go beyond the fountain and you'll see the entrance to the pool beside the SPA. Have a great time!

Mrs. Jones: Oh, one other thing. I need some sun block. Can I buy it here?

Jane: Yes, Ma'am. We have a little boutique that sells a variety of things. It is **directly back past** the front desk.

Mrs. Jones: Thank you so much. You have been very helpful!

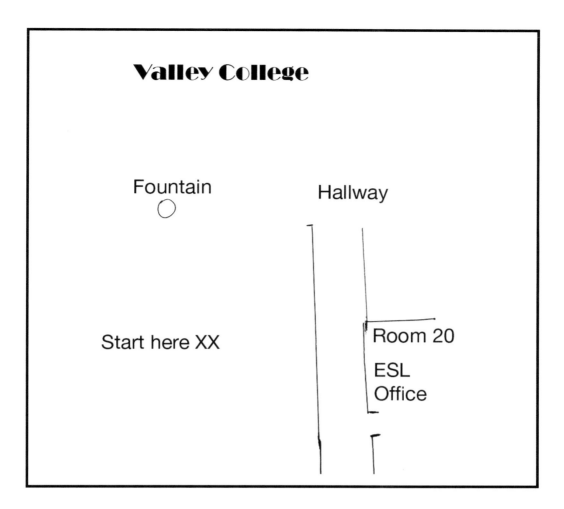

DIRECTIONS: *Please look at the map of the College and give the directions to the English as a Second Language office.*

New Student: Hi I'm new here. Could you tell me where the ESL office is?

Current Student: Absolutely. I'm happy to help you. You_____ go _____ ahead. Can you see the fountain? Turn_____ at the fountain and walk to the hallway. Turn right and go _____ the hall to room 20. That will be the ESL office, which will be on your _____.

Unit 7

SUCCESSFULLY RESOLVING CUSTOMER COMPLAINTS

We strive for perfection with all of our guest interactions and the delivery of our products. However, once in a while, our guest will not be happy with our service or product. In other words, things will "go wrong", at times, no matter where we work. We can turn the situation around to actually be a positive experience for our guest by using the best language and take the best action to solve the issue. This unit will equip you with the best approach with that unhappy guest. Let's always keep in mind that many times we have not been responsible for the problem, but we are the representative of the store or restaurant and must do everything to resolve the issue and ensure our guest will return.

Do we want our guests to complain?

A survey was conducted which asked guests if they would return to a restaurant or hotel based on the type of service or product they received. The goal of every business to ensure your customers return.

Companies **go out of business** (close) if their customers don't return.
Companies **stay in business** (stay open) if they have a
high percentage of returning customers.

(Try to guess the percentage of guests who returned to a hotel or restaurant after receiving various types of service.
Answers are on the next page. Talk with your partner before you turn the page.)

Type of Service of Guests Who Returned	**Percentage**
A.) Mr. and Mrs. Diaz had good service and no complaints at Piazza D'Angelo in Mill Valley. *(If everything goes well, what percentage of your guests will return?)*	_____%
B.) Mary and Alice had very slow service and over cooked fish at the Sausalito Grill. They didn't feel like telling the server about these issues, so there was no resolution. *(If there is a problem and nothing is done about it, what percentage of your guests will return?)*	_____%
C.) Sally's salmon was over cooked at the Seaview Restaurant. When she told the server, he apologized and offered to bring her another salmon. She said that would be fine. *(If there is a problem and it is resolved, what percentage of your guests will return?)*	_____%
D.) Jose found a shoe (not his) under his bed when he checked in to the Marin Hotel. The Housekeeping Manager apologized and sent a Room Attendant to clean his room again. She also sent a basket of fruit and a bottle of wine to his room with a note, apologizing again. *(If there is a problem that is resolved AND the guest is given something EXTRA, what percentage will return?)*	_____%

A. 94%   B. 23%   C. 79%   D. 98%

What did those percentages tell you? Do we want our guests to complain? We can see that when our customer complains, it's actually an opportunity to resolve an issue AND give them something special. Do you think they'll tell their friends about this great experience? Absolutely!

The Most Gracious English Will Help You Take Care of Your Unhappy Guest

(And remember Unit 2 on Body Language! You are going to use all of that now!)

1.) Apologize-It is probably not your fault but you are the representative of your hotel or restaurant. Your guest wants to hear that someone cares. An apology is a good beginning. Here are some good examples:

  a.) I am very sorry.
  b.) I understand how upset you must be.
  c.) I understand how you feel.
  d.) This is certainly not up to our standards.

2.) Listen (don't interrupt)- Most people want to vent (talk about their problem) when they are upset. Allow your guest to tell you what happened and how they feel. Listen actively. (See lesson 2 on Body language.)

3.) Offer a Solution- If possible, offer a choice of solutions. If the fish was over cooked, offer a replacement or a completely different item from the menu. **Do not make excuses or blame others. The guest doesn't want to hear about lack of staffing or other issues. For example, never say, "A lot of people called in sick today." Or "The chef has been making mistakes tonight." It is not professional to share workplace problems with your customers.**

  a.) May I offer you another steak or would you like to see the menu again? I will ensure this is cooked perfectly.

  b.) I will also ensure that this is taken care of immediately. I will **expedite** *this for you.*

4.) Offer something EXTRA- this will ensure that your customer returns!!

I'd like to <u>make this up to you</u>. May I offer you _____ or would you like _____. I'd like to give you something that you would appreciate and is exactly what you would like.

(Offer something that is meaningful to the guest. Be sure your restaurant, hotel, or store approves of what you are giving the guest. Here are some ideas: glass or bottle of wine, dessert, appetizer, complimentary dinner, complimentary room, or a spa treatment.)

5.) <u>Thank your customer</u> for telling you about this problem. –Think of a complaint as an <u>opportunity</u> to fix something and WOW your guest by making it up to them.

You are very important to us. We value your opinion. Thank you for telling us about this.

We value you as a customer. Thank you.

Is This Customer Satisfied?

Mr. and Mrs. Vega have been looking forward to eating at the Prime Steakhouse for several weeks. When Mr. Vega made the reservation, he mentioned that they would be celebrating their anniversary. Let's listen to their experience.

Host (Manager) - Welcome to the Prime Steakhouse. Do you have a reservation?

Mr. Vega- Yes. Mr. and Mrs. Vega.

Host- Oh, yes. We have a nice table for you by the window or would you prefer the middle section?

Mr. Vega- Oh, we'd like the window, wouldn't we, honey?

Mrs. Vega- Yes, that's fine.

Mr. and Mrs. Vega each order the New York steaks. Mr. Vega orders his medium and Mrs. Vega orders hers rare. They are enjoying a nice bottle of Cabernet Sauvignon and are very happy with the restaurant. Everything seems to be going well. They ordered their steaks at about 7:30pm. It is now about 8pm.

Mr. Vega- Gee, honey, our dinner seems to be taking a long time. I wonder if everything is OK? Our waiter did seem a bit rushed when he took our order, but I really like the atmosphere here. I'm going to ask our waiter what is going on.

Mrs. Vega- Yes, I am starting to get really hungry.

Mr. Vega- (to the server) – Is there some problem? We ordered our steaks more than a half an hour ago.

Server- Oh, yeah. I'll check.

The server does not return to their table for at least ten minutes.

Server- The steaks will be here soon. We had a lot of people call in sick tonight. Can't you see how busy I am?

Mr. Vega- My wife is getting very hungry. You are not being very helpful. I'd like to talk to your manager.

Server- Sure, no problem.

Mr. Vega- *(very upset)* No problem? Yes, there most certainly **is** a problem!!

Manager- What do you want?

Mr. Vega- We have been waiting for...........

Manager- *(He interrupts Mr. Vega)* Oh, we have been really busy tonight and we had.......

Mr. Vega- would you let me finish. My wife and I came out for a very special dinner and we have had to wait for about 45 minutes for our steaks. Doesn't that seem **outrageous** to you?

Manager- *(He looks at the floor when he is talking)* Not really. You see, you have to understand that we didn't expect this many customers and our chef is slammed. There's really nothing I can do about it. **(His arms are crossed in front of him.)**

Mr. Vega- You know, we came here in a very good mood to celebrate a very special occasion and now you have ruined it. We are leaving now and, believe me, we will tell our friends to stay away from this place!! We were going to have our daughter's wedding reception here, but we certainly won't be doing that now!! Come on, Honey. There are plenty of other restaurants on 4th Street. We'll just go down the block.

DISCUSS: What are three things you would tell the manager to do to ensure these customers return to this restaurant?
What are three things you would tell the server?

Is This Customer Satisfied?

Mr. and Mrs. Vega have been looking forward to eating at the Park Grill for several weeks. When Mr. Vega made the reservation, he mentioned that they would be celebrating their anniversary. Let's listen to their experience.

Host (Manager) - Welcome to the Park Grill. Do you have a reservation?

Mr. Vega- Yes. Mr. and Mrs. Vega.

Host- Oh, yes. We have a nice table for you by the window or would you prefer the middle section?

Mr. Vega- Oh, we'd like the window, wouldn't we, honey?

Mrs. Vega- Yes, that's fine.

Mr. and Mrs. Vega each order the New York steaks. Mr. Vega orders his medium and Mrs. Vega orders hers rare. Everything seems to be going well.

Server- Mr. and Mrs. Vega, I know you ordered your steaks about 20 minutes ago but it is going to be just a little longer. I am very sorry for the delay.

Mr. Vega- Oh, that's OK. Thank you for telling us.

Ten more minutes go by........

Mrs. Vega- Oh, honey, I am getting hungry.

Mr. Vega- Yes. I am going to speak to the manager.

Manager- How may I help you?

Mr. Vega- Well, our server very politely told us there was a delay with our dinner but this has been taking too long. We are here for a special occasion and I don't think we should have to wait so long.

Manager *(he makes good eye contact with the Vegas)* - Yes, Mr. Vega. I am very sorry. I certainly understand how you feel. We know you are here for your special anniversary. This is not up to our standards. We would like to make this up to you. May I offer you a complimentary bottle of wine or would you like a complimentary dessert? I will also **expedite** your order.

Mr. Vega- Well, honey, what would you like?

Mrs. Vega- I think the wine would be nice.

Manager- Very good. I'll have that sent right over.

Mr. Vega- Thank you very much. I really appreciated the fact that you actually listened to me. That means a lot.

Manager- We really value you as a customer. We want to ensure that everything is perfect for you. When it is not, we want to make it right for you.

Their steaks and wine arrive within a few minutes. After they have started eating, the server comes to their table.

Server- Again, we apologize for the delay. How is the wine and your meal?

Mr. Vega- Everything is wonderful! We are going to tell all of our friends about this experience and tell them they have to come here!! You really went beyond our expectations!

DISCUSS: Compare the experience at the Park Grill with the experience at the Prime Steakhouse. What was the difference in actions, words, body language, and attitude toward the customer?

What would be your response to these situations?

Situation 1: You are the restaurant manager. The guest has told you that the service in the restaurant is very slow and inattentive. They said they have been waiting twenty minutes for their appetizers and they are very upset. (Three servers called in sick tonight and you couldn't get any replacements).

I'm terribly sorry. This is not up to our standards. I will take care of this right away. Let me expedite your order for you. And I'd also like to offer you a complimentary glass of wine or a dessert, if you'd like, to make up for this.

Situation 2: You are a front desk agent. The guest called the front desk and said they found a used washcloth in the bathroom after they checked in to their guest room. What would you say to the guest?

Oh, I am very sorry. I understand how upset you must be. We have very high standards of cleanliness and this should not have happened. Please allow me to fix this problem. May I send a Room Attendant to clean your bathroom again and bring you a fresh washcloth? Would it be convenient for her to clean now? I would also like to offer you a complimentary breakfast in our Garden Restaurant or may I offer you a complimentary bottle of wine and cheese platter to be sent to your room? Again, we are very sorry this happened.

Situation 3: You are a server in a seafood restaurant. The customer told you that the fish is overcooked and dry.

I am very sorry about this. Please let me replace that with another salmon or would you like something else? I will expedite your order so that you do not have to wait long at all. Please let us make this up to you. We won't charge you for this. It will be "on the house" with our sincerest apologies!

Situation 4- The customer's water glass has lipstick on it.

I'm so sorry. Please let me get you a clean one. Thank you for pointing that out to me. May I get you a complimentary glass of wine?

Scenarios for an unhappy guest
Work with your partner as a guest or employee in each scenario.

Situation 1: The service in the restaurant is very slow and inattentive.
You are very upset about this. No one has taken your order and you have been there for twenty minutes. You are in the restaurant for a special occasion. It is your spouse's birthday. You told them this when you made the reservation, but no one has acknowledged this. You feel that they don't care about you. You are VERY angry!! The manager will probably apologize but you continue to be angry until you feel they have "bent over backwards" to please you.

Situation 2: You found a used washcloth in the bathroom after you checked in to your guest room.
You are now wondering if this hotel is clean. You are thinking of moving to another hotel. Do you think the housekeeping supervisor cares about you? Are they making you feel special? You continue to threaten to leave the hotel until they do something to make you feel special.

Situation 3: The fish is overcooked and dry.
You had to wait a very long time for your meal and now it is overcooked. You are thinking of leaving this restaurant and going to another one down the street. Do you think the restaurant manager cares about you? Do you think you will ever return to this restaurant? If the manager makes you feel special, then you might consider returning.

Situation 4: You found dried toothpaste in the sink in the bathroom when you checked in to your room.
You are wondering if this is a clean hotel. Does the housekeeping manager care about you? Will you return to this hotel? You remain angry until the manager does something to make you feel special.

<u>Responses to an Unhappy Guest</u>

<u>Situation 1:</u> You are the manager of a large restaurant.

You are having a difficult night. Three servers have called in sick and you could not find replacements. It is a busy Friday night with many customers. Some guests seem to be waiting a long time for service. What can you do? Remember to use some of the ideas on pages 39 and 40. Don't forget to apologize and offer some EXTRA item to make the guest feel special. Tell them how much you value them as a customer.

<u>Situation 2:</u> You are the Housekeeping Manager.

You have gone to the guest's room because they have told you that they found a used washcloth in their bathroom when they checked in to their room. It is important to apologize and make this guest feel special. Be sure to empathize with the guest and use the ideas on pages 39 and 40 to convey your apologies.

<u>Situation 3:</u> You are server at a popular seafood restaurant.

It has been a very busy night. The guest ordered his sword fish rare and you are sure you wrote that on the order but the chef overcooked it. How will you make this up to the guest? You want to be sure that this unhappy guest returns to your restaurant. Remember to offer something of value to make up for this. Use some of the ideas on pages 39 and 40.

<u>Situation 4:</u> You are the Housekeeping Manager at a busy hotel.

You want to ensure that this guest returns to your hotel. What will you do? Use some of the ideas on pages 39 and 40.

Unit 8

PROFESSIONAL ENGLISH FOR PHONE INTERACTIONS

Communicating effectively by phone presents special challenges when interacting with your customers in a second language. The following qualities are always important, but even more so, when we remove "face-to face" facial expressions and only communicate with our voice and words. Let's consider these qualities: (Don't worry; we'll have an opportunity to practice all of them!)

a.) **Positive tone of voice-** Your voice should be in a medium range; not too low or too high. The tone should convey energy and enthusiasm. Have a smile in your voice.

b.) **Clarity of spoken words-** Try to enunciate as clearly as you can. Speaking a little slower than you normally do is OK. Always use professional, gracious English; no slang please!

c.) Listen fully- Avoid interrupting or talking over your customer. Even if you think you know what they are going to say, let them finish their sentences.

d.) Use customer's name- When you find out the name of your customer, use it in a natural manner at least twice. Address your customer as Mr. Mrs. or Ms. with their last name.

e.) Be sincere- Respond to your customer with a caring quality in your voice; NOT in a robotic, mechanical way. Treat your customer as an individual; not a "one-size-fits-all" kind of response.

f.) Have paper and pen ready- Be ready to write down any information that may be pertinent to your discussion, so that your customer does not have to repeat themselves.

g.) Leave your customer satisfied- Be sure your customer understands everything you have discussed. Check with them by repeating or giving an overall summery of the points of the call and how it was resolved. Don't hang up until your customer is satisfied and pleased.

PRACTICE- Let's try to identify the qualities above as we practice the best (or not!) way to give our best service over the phone.

Joe is a Customer Service Agent for an on-line hardware store. Let's listen as he "helps" a customer.

(Ring, ring, ring, ring, ring............)

Joe- (chewing gum) Hello, Marin Hardware.

Mr. Thompson (customer) - Oh, yes. I received two invoices for the same thing- a stepladder- can you help me?

Joe- Oh, yea. I guess so. Um...your name?

Mr. Thompson- Thompson. James Thompson.

Joe- OK. Invoice number? Oh, and, you know you can do all this on our website. You don't have to call.

Mr. Thompson- I'd rather not use the compu......... (Joe interrupts him...

Joe- (sounding exasperated) Oh, OK ...What is the invoice number? Can't you see it? It's right there.

Mr. Thompson- No. I can't find it.

Joe- It's on the right.

Mr. Thompson- Oh, yes. Now I see it. It's 473021.

Joe- (he wasn't ready to write or input the number) What was that again?

Mr. Thompson- 473021

Joe- OK. Now I can see the two invoices. I'll cancel one, but you need to pay the other one. OK, next time use the website. (Mumbled so that Mr. Thompson had a hard time understanding him.)

Mr. Thompson- What did you say? (Now there is no answer. Joe has hung up!!)

DISCUSS- Talk about this phone interaction with your partner using points a-g above. What "grade" would you give Joe?

PRACTICE- Let's try another example.

(Ring, ring)
Maria- (With a smile in her voice.) Thank you for calling Marin Hardware. Maria speaking. How may I help you today?

Mrs. Jones- My name is Mary Jones and it looks like I have received two bills for the same thing. I ordered a stepladder from your website on December 5th and charged it on my store credit card.

Maria- Oh, yes, I'd be happy to help you with that, Mrs. Jones. First I want to apologize on behalf of all of us here at Marin Hardware. We pride ourselves on being accurate with our billing procedures, but it looks like we made a mistake.

Mrs. Jones- Oh, I understand.

Maria- Let's see... is your address still on Sir Francis Drake?

Mrs. Jones- Yes, that's correct.

Maria- Good, Mrs. Jones. And would you, by any chance, have the invoice number available? It is located in the upper right corner of your bill.

Mrs. Jones- Oh, let's see. Oh, yes, here it is. It's 74209.

Maria- Great. That was 74209. Correct?

Mrs. Jones- Yes, that's right.

Maria- Oh, yes, now I see there is a double billing for you. Again, we are so sorry. I'll remove that from your store credit card. Would you prefer a confirmation of this credit sent to your email address or your home address?

Mrs. Jones- My home address please. I really don't like to do very much on my computer.

Maria- Well, that's fine, Mrs. Jones. That's why we're here. We like to talk to our customers.

Mrs. Jones- Thank you very much. You have been very helpful.

Maria- It has been my pleasure. May I help you with anything else today?

Mrs. Jones- No, that will be all.

Maria- I hope I have explained everything clearly. You will be receiving your confirmation of the cancelled invoice in the mail. We want to thank you for choosing Marin Hardware. We'd like to send you a $20.00 gift card as our way of apologizing for our billing mistake.

Mrs. Jones- Thank you so much. Very kind of you.

Unit 9

<u>BRAINSTORMING</u>

Free your mind to get your most creative ideas

How many times have you tried to solve a problem and have felt you were getting nowhere? You just kept coming back to the same ineffectual ideas. Well, we're going to try a new approach. It's called brainstorming.

The concept of "freeing your thoughts" or brainstorming was created in 1953 by Madison Avenue advertising executive Alex Osborn. It basically encourages people to approach a problem by presenting thoughts and ideas that can, at first, seem a bit crazy. A simultaneous goal is that one idea can spark another. This helps to get people "unstuck" by jolting them out of their normal ways of thinking. The phrase "**Think outside the box**" was a direct result of this approach.

Let's Practice Effective Brainstorming

1.) Gather in a group of three or more in a relatively quiet and comfortable area. Materials needed are "Post-its", pens, and a whiteboard or flip chart. If you have to limit your time, choose a "timekeeper".

2.) Choose your target problem or issue. Present the problem clearly. Emphasize the goal is to get as many ideas as possible.

3.) **All ideas are welcome**. There are no "stupid" ideas. Quirky ideas are welcome. Avoid criticizing or rewarding ideas. You want to open all possibilities. You don't want to limit any idea.

4.) Give people time to think on their own.

5.) **Begin by writing each of your ideas on a "Post-it".***** After everyone has at least written one idea, share (talk about) your ideas and attach them to your board or flip chart. Use and develop ideas to create or spark new ones. Encourage the "quiet" people to contribute.

6.) Evaluate the ideas at the end of the session. Choose the best idea and present it to the class. Then, you can also present all of the ideas to the class.

***Another approach, at this point, is to allow all to _verbally_ express their ideas. A designated member of the group will write them on the board as they are offered.

Brainstorming Projects

Let's Find a Solution Together

Directions: Using the guidelines above, work with your group to find the best solutions to the following problems. Remember the key is to free your thoughts!! Be creative!! All ideas are welcome!!

1.) **Marin County**: It has been observed that the roads in Marin County are in terrible condition. There are many potholes which can create a dangerous condition. What are your suggestions to alleviate this problem?

2.) **College of Marin**: There is no food available on campus for the students who attend classes on Saturdays. Many of the classes are three or four hours long. What are your suggestions to remedy this situation?

3.) **Supermarket**: Morale is low among the employees at this supermarket. Employees don't feel appreciated by their managers. Consequently, they arrive late and take longer breaks than allowed. What can you suggest to help them feel better about working there?

4.) **A Home improvement Center:** Customers complain that the employees are not helpful, not well-informed, and unfriendly. What ideas do you have to help this company?

5.) **At a Bank:** Customers seem confused when they enter bank. How would you help the bank solve this problem?

Unit 10
THE FINER POINTS OF GRAMMAR

This unit will focus on ensuring we are not only friendly, gracious, knowledgeable, and engaging, but that we use the English language correctly. The following focuses on the most commonly heard mistakes and how to avoid them.

1.   Gerunds and infinitives can be confusing:

Polite Requests with Gerunds

The following polite requests are followed by <u>gerunds:</u>

May I suggest **applying** for this position immediately?
Would you mind **waiting** just a few minutes while we set your table?
I would suggest **getting** an early start. The traffic will be terrible.

DIRECTIONS: Underline the gerund in the following sentences:

1.   Would you mind waiting here for a few minutes?
2.   May I recommend ordering the salmon? It's our specialty.
3.   I'd suggest arriving about twenty minutes early to avoid standing in line. Sundays are always busy.
4.   I'll finish setting this table in just a few minutes.

Practice: Use the polite requests above with your partner in the following situations:

1.) Your customer wants some help choosing the best wine.
2.) Your bank is very busy and you have to ask your customer to wait in line until the next bank teller is available.
3.) You politely say goodbye to your customer.

Use of Infinitives

1. Allow me **to show** you the way.
2. Allow me **to escort** you.
3. Let's plan **to start** the music at 8pm.
4. I hope you decided **to have** the special tonight.

2. Indirect pronouns

)The following verbs have an indirect pronoun immediately following them or at the end of the sentence.
offer
give
bring
get

May I offer **you** the menu?
May I offer the menu to **you**?

May I give **you** the check?
May I give the check to **you**?

May I get **you** a drink?
May I get a drink for **you**?

The following verbs have **no** indirect pronoun or only **at the end** of the sentence.
recommend
suggest

May I suggest the steak? It's our specialty.
May I suggest the steak **for you**?

May I recommend the chocolate cake? It's very popular.
May I recommend the chocolate cake **to you?**

1.) Use the following verbs with your partner.

      a. offer
      b. give
      c. bring
      d. get
      e. recommend
      f. suggest
      g. allow

2.) Use of "do" and "would"

"Would" in the following questions is used to find out if the person wants this now. You are offering this to your customer or co-worker.

Would you like coffee?
Would you like some more coffee? I just made a fresh pot.
Would you like dessert? We have the best apple pie in town.
Would you like this for here or to go?

"Do" in the following questions is used to find out if a person _likes_ something in general, but not if they _want_ it now.

Examples:

*Do you **like** sad movies? Yes, I do. Or No, I don't.*
*Do you **like** hot weather? Yes, I do. or _____*
*Do you **like** coffee in the morning? _____ or _____*
Do can be used with want if you are offering something, but the form above using would is more polite.

Do you want coffee?
Do you want some wine?
Do you want an appetizer?

PRACTICE:

Offer the following items to your partner:

1. Tea

2. Ice cream

3. Milk

4. Water

5. This sweater in a medium or large size

Ask you partner if they **like** the following:

1. Hot weather

2. Loud music

3. Puppies

4. Studying English

5. Cold weather

3.) **We like the sound of our name.**

Can you remember a recent experience when the salesperson used your name? How did you feel? How can we find out our customer's name? Please take a few minutes with your partner to brainstorm creative ideas.

Mrs. Jones (only use "Mrs." with the last name, ***never just "Mrs.")***
Mr. Jones (only use "Mr." with the last name, ***never just "Mr.")***
Ms. Jones (pronounced "MIZ", if we don't know if the woman is married or not)
Miss Jones (if you know the woman is not married)

If we don't know our customer's name, the following are the best "forms of address" to use:

Women

a.) Ma'am (originally Madam primarily used in England)

b.) Miss (for women under 30 or women of any age)

c.) Ladies (only used in the plural form for two or more women in a group; ***NOT used in the singular "lady".***)

Men

a.) Sir

b.) Gentlemen (used with two or more men who are together in a group.)

c.) For a group of men and women together the best is:

"How is **everyone** tonight?"

"Hi **guys"** is used frequently, but is casual language. It is not the most gracious or polite when you want to give the very best customer service.

Practice: Practice with your partner.

1. Two women enter your restaurant. You don't know their names.

   Example: Welcome, **ladies.** Would you like a table by the window or in the center?

2. Mr. Rodriguez, a customer who has been coming to your restaurant for two years, enters your restaurant. You know his name.

   Hello,_____. It is nice to see you again.

3. A group of men and women enter your store.

   Welcome! How is_____ today?

4. You are offering a table to a woman who is by herself.

   _____, would you like to sit here or would you like the table near the window?

5. Indirect Questions

An indirect question sounds more polite than a direct question. _Please note the change in syntax when asking an indirect question._

Direct question:	What do you want to eat?
Indirect question (more polite):	Have you decided what **you** would like to eat?
Direct question:	Where is the nearest gas station?
Indirect Question:	Can you tell me where the nearest gas station **is**?
Direct:	What time are you checking out?
Indirect question	May I ask you what time **you** are checking out?

The following are polite phrases to begin an indirect question:

1. Can you tell me...............
2. How can I ....
3. Do you know where............
4. Could you tell me where...............
5. Could you tell me how...............
6. Could you tell me when.............
7. Have you decided.............
8. May I ask you...............

PRACTICE: Use the expressions above with your partner.

Unit 11

TEAMWORK AND ATTITUDE

Teamwork and Attitude

What is good teamwork?

1. **Good Communication**
   - **Talk to co-workers politely**
   - **Offer help-Are you OK? Do you need some help?**
   - **Give good advice**
   - **Warn of potential problems**

2. **Working in a Group**

    - **Cooperate with co-workers**
    - **Focus on your job duties while being respectful of your co-workers.**
    - **Every job is important.**

3. **Respect each other**

    - **Don't argue**
    - **Don't gossip**
    - **Listen to new ideas**

4. **Give each other good ideas**

    - **Don't be afraid to suggest new ideas**
    - **Take a risk**
    - **Feel free to express yourself**

5. **Help each other**

    - **Keep in mind that a hotel or restaurant cannot be successful without the positive contributions of everyone on the team.**

6. **Respect the rules**

    - **The rules are for everyone.**

7. **Share supplies and resources**

    - **Be generous with everyone. You may need their help later!**

8. **Be fair**

    - **Treat everyone the way you would like to be treated!**

Teamwork and Attitude

Your attitude is the one thing that you can change. It is totally up to you.

Good teamwork is an important part of a good attitude. You should go to work with the idea that you want your customer to have a great experience and be willing to do "whatever it takes" to do that. You can feel positive and energized because you are creating a great experience for your customers. Most important – a hotel, restaurant or store cannot be successful without a great team!! The following are some good suggestions for good team work and attitude:

1. Try to offer to help a co-worker BEFORE they ask you. If you see someone that needs your help, offer it.
2. Compliment others when you see they are doing a good job. "I really like the way you handled that situation, Sue. The guest seemed really happy."
3. Ask for help if you need it. Your co-workers may not know you need help. It's OK to ask.
4. Don't gossip about co-workers.
5. Offer to work overtime, if your manager needs your help.
6. Keep a positive attitude. Don't complain about small inconveniences. Be positive about the food and service at your hotel or restaurant.
7. Offer to help your manager with special projects.
8. Try to do more than your job requires every day. Try to go "above and beyond".
9. Don't "disappear".

What would you do?

1. A co-worker has called in sick and Ellen (a Server) needs help in her section.
2. A co-worker has a lot of orders.
3. The manager needs people to work overtime.
4. The coffee maker in your section is broken and you have to walk a longer distance to get coffee for your customers.
5. A guest needs some help with directions to the closest gas station.
6. You see that Sue is helping a guest with her elderly mother.
7. You have suddenly become very busy and are having a difficult time keeping up with everything you have to do.

Who has a good attitude?

Sam- I just started working here a week ago and I really like it here.

Jane- Oh, yeah? It's OK. The customers can be a bother sometimes. The food is usually too salty. Our manager is really strict. He won't let me listen to my IPOD when I'm serving. The other servers are a bunch of snobs.

Sam- Well, I'll have to see about that. I think every customer is a good customer because if they were not here, we wouldn't have a job.

Jane- OK. You can think whatever you want.

Later that night Sam's section is very busy with a lot of special orders.

Sam- I wonder where Jane is. I could really use her help. Oh, there she is.

Jane, could you help me take these food orders to table 15?

Jane- I don't think so. I have to check on <u>my</u> customers.

Sam- It doesn't look like you are very busy.

Jane- I'm not. I just don't believe in teamwork. My philosophy is every man for himself!!

It's great to have a positive attitude and good teamwork

John is a new busser at the **Prime Steakhouse.** *He has received one week of training and this is his first day on the job.*

John- Hi, Ellen. I'm a little nervous. This is my first day here at the Prime Steakhouse. I hope I don't make any mistakes.

Ellen (Server) - Oh, I remember my first few weeks here. I was nervous, too. You know, the thing I remember the most was how helpful everyone was. They are still very helpful!

John- We had a week of training but I don't know if I'll remember everything.

Ellen- I'll help you. There is a lot to learn. One of the most important things to remember is to smile and always be polite and pleasant with our customers. If you don't remember what to do, just ask me. I will be happy to help you. I would rather that you ask me about something than try to guess. If you really don't know, that is OK. It would be worse to do it wrong.

John pours water for a party of four but forgets the bread.

Ellen- John, let me help you. Did you forget the bread and butter for table 14?

John- Oh, I'm sorry. Another guest asked me for something and I guess I forgot.

Ellen- That's O.K. I took care of it for you. Part of our job is remembering a lot of things. We are on our way to do something and a customer will ask us for something else. It happens all the time and is part of the job. There's a lot going on!

John- Thanks, Ellen. I won't forget it again!

Ellen- We're a team. **I've got your back!!** The most important thing about good teamwork is that we look out for each other. If I need help, I know I can count on you to help me. If you need help, you can **rely** on me to help you. I have worked at some restaurants where there is too much competition.

John- Oh, I know what that's like. I worked in a place where no one helped anyone else. Everyone was trying to outdo each other. It was terrible.

Later that night Ellen has a table with a party of eight that is keeping her quite busy along with her other tables. She needs help.

John- I see that you have a very busy table over there. **I'm all caught up with my tables**. I'll help you bring out the entrees for the party of eight.

Ellen- Oh, thanks, John. That is great teamwork!

Unit 12
SUCCESSFUL INTERVIEWS AND RESUMES

Important Interview Tips

1. **Dress appropriately**- It is important to make a good first impression. Your clothes are a reflection of you. Conservative dress is best. For men, it is a good idea to wear a tie and jacket and be sure your shoes are shined. For women, it is best to wear a conservative pants suit or a suit with a skirt with conservative earrings.

2. **Positive body language** – Always start the interview with a smile and a firm hand shake. Make good eye-contact, listen carefully, and maintain good posture throughout the interview. .

3. **Good Grooming**- Ensure that your hair and nails are clean. Proper hygiene is essential.

4. **Resume**- It is important to have a resume. Ensure that it is up-to-date. Enlist a friend or relative to "proofread" it to ensure there are no grammatical errors. Examples of good resumes are on the following pages.

5. **Examples**- When answering questions, always give **specific examples. Don't generalize**.

   Generalized statement: "I am really organized."

   Specific example: (bus person) "My previous manager said I was really organized. For example, I always kept our supply area well stocked, without being reminded. The servers were always happy when I was working with them."

6. **Be knowledgeable about the job**- Try to find out exactly what the job you are interviewing for entails. This will be important when you are interviewing.

7. **Practice** your interview with a family member or friend. Use the list of typical interview questions provided on the next page. **Speak clearly and confidently**.

8. **Questions**- Always ask good questions related to the job you are interviewing for.

9. **Be knowledgeable** about the company you are interviewing with. Try to do some research on the internet or by asking people who work there.

10. **Don't** ask about salary, hours, benefits, vacation time, or background checks. The interviewer will probably tell you all of these things. Allow them to bring up these topics.

11. **Speak positively**- It is OK to speak positively about yourself. You can say, "My manager said I was organized." Or you can say, **"My co-workers said I was very reliable."**

12. **Listen carefully**- It is very important to listen to the interviewer's questions and answer them carefully. Allow them to finish asking the question before you answer it.

13. **Be punctual and do not bring family members or friends with you.** – It is best to arrive a little early for the interview.

14. **Follow-up**- It is important to write a short thank you note or email to reiterate your interest in the job.

15. **Be polite to the receptionist.**

Typical Interview Questions

Use this list to practice for your interview. It is best to practice with a friend or family member. Be prepared with your own examples BEFORE you go to the interview. This will help you to stay calm and feel more confidant. Remember the interviewer might interview several people for this job, so you want to be sure you make the best impression. You want to separate yourself from the other candidates.

1.) **"Can you tell me about your work background?"** Or **"Can you tell me about your background?"** *(Your interviewer wants to hear about your work history, not about your personal life. This is sometimes called an **Elevator Speech**, because it should be about two minutes, at the most – an average elevator ride- and keep it positive and to the point. Here is an example:*

"My first job was at a small restaurant in Guatemala, which is where I am from. I started as a general helper and then I was promoted to be a server. Then, shortly after I moved here, I worked at Safeway in the bakery department. That was a really great experience. I learned a lot about the importance of teamwork and being reliable. My current job is at Office Depot, where I enjoy helping customers with anything they need."

2. **What experience have you had that would make you good for this job?**

The Best Answer-

If you have had the exact job that you are interviewing for, tell about **specific details** of that job.

"I was a bus person at the Prime Burger Restaurant for three years. **All the servers said I was the most helpful bus person. For example, I always organized the supplies in my free time, without being reminded. I know how to use my time well and work in a busy restaurant."**

(This is a good answer because you have given the interviewer some exact examples to help them remember you. They will be impressed!)

If you do not have direct experience in that exact job, then be prepared with examples that **relate** to the job you are interviewing for. We call those transferable skills.

"I worked in the delivery area of the 7-11 store. I had to be very organized and meet deadlines everyday. I also worked with a variety of people and helped our customers. My manager said the customers thought I was very friendly and efficient. **I think those are the qualities of a good bus person."**

Don't forget to include work experience from your country.

The Worst Answer- "I don't have any. I just need a job. I am an organized person."
(This is not a good answer because you have not given a specific example. Your interviewer will not be impressed because you have been too general.)

3. **Why do you want to work here?**

Best answer-
"I have heard this is a wonderful (restaurant, store, hotel). **I would be proud to work here.**

Worst answer- Because I need a job.

4. **Can you tell me of a time when you went above and beyond; when you did more than was expected of you?**

Best answer-
"Yes. At my last job, a customer left their child's sweater at the restaurant. They needed it right away. I was going home in the direction of their house and delivered it to them. **They were very grateful!**"

(Be prepared with an example from any of your past jobs.)

Worst answer- I can't think of anything.

5. **Can you tell me about a time when you had to deal with a crisis or an unhappy customer?**

Best answer-
(in a hotel) "Yes. A guest told me that her air conditioning was not working. She was very upset. I told her I would take care of it. I reported it, made sure it was fixed, and sent her an apology note with a basket of fruit. The guest was very pleased and has returned to our hotel. **I took ownership of the problem.**"

(Be prepared with an example).

Worst answer- I can't think of anything.

6. **Why do you want to leave the job you have now?**

Best answer-
"Well, I like it there, but I really want a **bit more of a challenge** and I have heard very good things about this_____.

Worst answer-
"I really don't like the place I am working now. They don't treat me very well and I don't like the people I work with."

Practice Interviews

With a partner, practice answering the following interview questions. Remember to be specific. You are interviewing for a job that you would be interested in now.

The job you are interviewing for is_____.
(server, sales clerk, day care manager, etc.)

1. **Could you tell me about yourself?**
   OR
   Could you tell me about your background?
   (Elevator speech)

2. **What were your main responsibilities (or duties) in your last job or your current job?**

3. **Why do you think you would be good for this job?**

4. **Have you ever done more than your job required?**

5. **What are your strengths? What are your best work abilities and personal qualities?**

6. **Have you ever had to deal with an unhappy customer?**

7. **Have you ever had a conflict with a co-worker?**

8. **Why do you want to work here?**

9. **Why do you want to leave your current job?**

10. **Can you work flexible hours?**

11. **When can you start?**

12. **We pay $_____ an hour.**

Would You Hire John?

John is interviewing for a position as a busperson at the **Prime Steakhouse.** *He hasn't prepared for the interview and is very nervous. Let's listen to his interview.*

Mr. Jones (Manager) - Welcome, John. Thank you for coming in today.

John- (Does not make eye-contact and does not shake hands). Hello.

Mr. Jones- Do you have a resume?

John- Oh, I didn't think I would need one.

Mr. Jones- Well, let's get started. What is your past experience?

John- Well, I worked as a helper in a restaurant in my hometown. I really don't have much experience. I just need a job.

Mr. Jones- I see. Can you give me an example of when you went above and beyond in your job?

John- I really can't think of anything.

Mr. Jones- Why do you want to work here?

John- Oh, I guess it would be nice. As I said, I really need to work.

Mr. Jones- Have you worked in a busy atmosphere?

John- Well, yeah, I guess. In my other restaurant, people were always stressed out.

Mr. Jones- Well, I see. Do you have any questions for me?

John- Oh, yeah. When will I get a vacation? And what are the days off?

Mr. Jones- Well, we'll get to that if you are hired. Thank you for coming in today. We should be making our decision in the next week or so.

John- Thank you. Goodbye.

Would you Hire Henry?

Henry is interviewing for a bus person position at the **Prime Steakhouse.** *He has been practicing with his brother and he hopes he does well on the interview. Let's listen.*

Mr. Jones (Manager) - Welcome, Henry. Thank you for coming in today.

Henry- (Makes good eye contact with Mr. Jones and gives him a firm handshake). Thank you for seeing me, Mr. Jones.

Mr. Jones- May I see your resume?

Henry- Yes. Here it is. I also have a certificate from a special Customer Service course that I took at the College of Marin.

(Henry has good posture and good eye contact throughout the interview. He speaks in a clear voice.)

Mr. Jones- Thank you. That sounds like a great course. Tell me about your work experience.

Henry- In Mexico, which is where I am from, I worked at a well-known restaurant as a busperson. Since I have been here, I have been working at the Apple Café as a busperson. I really enjoy the restaurant business.

Mr. Jones- Great. Why do you think you would be good in this position?

Henry- I am efficient and thorough. My manager tells me that he can always rely on me to stay on top of things. The servers tell me that they are always happy when I am working because everything goes smoothly.

Mr. Jones- We have a very busy restaurant here. We are very popular. Do you think you can handle it?

Henry- Oh, yes. I am accustomed to a busy atmosphere. I enjoy it! I am organized and I keep calm.

Mr. Jones- Have you ever done more than your job required?

Henry- Yes. When I have extra time, I set up the supplies for the next day. Everyone says that has been a big help at the restaurant. I also help the guests with directions and I bring coloring books for their children.

Mr. Jones- That sounds good. Why do you want to leave your current job?

Henry- Well, I like it there, but I have heard that this is a very good restaurant. I would like a little bit more of a challenge.

Mr. Jones- Well, do you have any questions for me?

Henry- I have done a little research on your restaurant. It seems you are busy at all times of the year. Is that true?

Mr. Jones- Yes. We really don't have a slow period, thankfully.

Henry- That's great.

Mr. Jones- Thank you for coming in today. We should be making our decision next week.

Henry- Thank you, again. I really enjoyed meeting you and I am very interested in this position.

Sample Resume

John Smith
999 Main Street San Rafael, California 94904
Home Phone: (415) 999-4245 email: JSC@yahoo.com

Summary of Qualifications

- **Over eight years as a bus person and server in the restaurant industry.**
- **Solid knowledge of superior customer service.**
- **Well-organized with a proven ability to learn new tasks quickly.**
- **Excelled in specialized Hotel and Restaurant course at the College of Marin.**

Experience

Prime Steakhouse Restaurant 2008-Present
San Rafael, California
Bus person
Assist servers to ensure that guests receive the very highest level of service. Consistently exceeded guest's expectations in providing superior service as a bus person in obtaining water, bread, condiments, serving meals, pouring coffee, and clearing. Selected by the manager to perform the duties of a server when restaurant was especially busy.

La Vista Café 2002- 2006
Guatemala City
Server
Exceeded guest's expectations in providing quality service in taking orders and presenting meals in this highly regarded restaurant in Guatemala.

Education

Guatemala College 1999-2001

College of Marin 2010
Received Golden Certificate of Achievement in a specialized Customer Service course.

<u>Languages</u>

Spanish and English

References available upon request.

Unit 13
TRAITS OF GOOD MANAGERS AND GOOD EMPLOYEES

The Qualities of a Good Manager and Leader

1. Honesty
2. Fairness
3. Solid knowledge of the department
4. Ability to "pitch in" when necessary
5. Ability to encourage others
6. Be a good listener- show an understanding of an employee's point of view.
7. Promote teamwork
8. Show genuine appreciation for the work staff members do.
9. Give positive reinforcement- praise and compliments.

10. Be a good role model- One of the most popular sports is "watching the boss."

11. Ability to "think on your feet"; to think quickly to solve problems.

12. Emphasize the positive, not the negative.

13. Be respectful to everyone.

14. Be organized.

15. Stay calm and even-tempered.

Traits of Good Managers

1. Show Appreciation:

   a.)When you see your employee handle a difficult situation well:

   "That was great, Dora. I really liked the way you handled that customer/situation. Well done!!"

   b.)When an employee improves in any way:

   "I can see how much you have improved in the last few weeks. Thanks for going that extra mile!!"

   c.)After (or during) an especially difficult day:

   "I really want to thank you for all you have done today. This was a very challenging day for everyone. I want you to know how much I appreciate your ability to adapt to this situation! Outstanding!!"

2. Encourage Great Results

   a.) Please feel free to ask me any questions. I am here to help you succeed! I know you have received some training, but I understand not everything is always covered in our training presentation."

3. Be knowledgeable

   a.) Take whatever time necessary to know all the aspects of your workplace. Even if you have never actually performed the job you are managing, you must be aware of all that it entails.

4. Be Flexible

   a.) Know how to administer and regulate workplace procedures in a fair and reasonable manner.

5. <u>Encourage employee input (participation) for new ideas to improve workplace procedures and environment.</u>

"I really want to hear your opinion (or ideas) on how we should improve our_____. I have received some of the best ideas from you, our employees. You deal with this every day, so I think of you as the experts!!"

Is Robert a Good Manager?

Would you want to work at the Prime Steakhouse?

Robert- Hi. I am your new manager. I expect everyone to do a good job here.

Steve (bus person) – Welcome. We are happy to have you. Yes, everyone here is very proud of their jobs here

Robert-- Good. I have been watching the staff for a while. That guy over there looks like he's lazy. I am going to talk to him.

Robert (to Fred) - Hey, Fred, I'm the new manager and it looks like you haven't finished your work here. You'd better shape up or you will be out of here.

Fred- Yes, sir. I will finish it now. I just wanted to explain that a customer wanted.......

Robert- I don't want to listen to excuses. Just get busy.

Later that day........

Robert- I can't believe this staff. They aren't very good. I know it's a busy day but... I think I'll go out and have a smoke.

Steve- Wow, that new manager is so negative. All of our customers are having a great time and the chef is doing a fantastic job on the busy day. We are all pulling together and working well as a team.

Fred- Yes, he just doesn't seem to like me.

Steve- Can you believe that he is outside during our busiest time? Our other manager would be here helping with everything---pitching in.

An hour later......

Robert- Well, it's still busy here. I guess the customers like it here.

Sylvia- Hi, John. I am happy to see a new manager. You seem like you will be very good. I was wondering if I could leave early today? I have a hair appointment that I just can't miss.

Robert- Sure. Why not?

Steve- I can't believe he let Silvia go early on such a busy day. That is really not fair.

Fred- I don't think this manager is going to last very long here.

Is Joe a Good Manager?

Would you want to work at the Park Grill Restaurant?

Joe- Hi. I am your new manager. I have a great deal of respect for all of you. This is an excellent restaurant and I am very happy to be here. I want to get to know all of you.

Steve (bus person) – Welcome. We are happy to have you. Yes, everyone here is very proud of their jobs here

Joe- Good. I have been watching the staff for a while. Everyone looks like they work well as a team. That is very important.

A little later.................

Joe (to Fred) - Hi, Fred, I'm the new manager and it looks like you haven't been able to finish your work here. I saw you were helping that guest and got a little behind. Do you need some help?

Fred- Yes, sir. I will finish it now.

Joe- I understand. I will help you and I will ask Sylvia to help you, also. She is not busy now.

Later that day........

Joe- Thanks again, Silvia, for helping Fred. That was great teamwork.

Sylvia- Oh, you are welcome. It is so nice to be appreciated. Oh, we have more customers than we expected. I really like the way you were able to think on your feet and rearrange the staffing for today.

Joe- Oh, yes. I am accustomed to turning on a dime in the restaurant business.

An hour later......

Joe- Well, it's still busy. I guess the customers like it here. I am going to make sure that all the staff get a special commendation in their file for working so well on such a busy day.

Steve- Great, Joe. We are happy to see a new manager. You seem like you will be very good. You really promote good teamwork.

Joe- Well, I believe in promoting a positive work environment. It makes it better for our employees and our guests.

Unit 14

<u>ECONOMICS</u>

<u>Unit 14 Let's talk about the Bottom Line: Economics in the Workplace</u>

At this point in our semester, it is time to talk about money. Unless you are a non-profit organization (charity, church, public clinic, volunteer services, museums, research institute), the goal of your company is to turn a profit (make money). Let's examine some aspects of this.

A.) *Pricing- How are goods (products) priced?*

    1.) *Several factors are involved in determining how much an item will cost.*

        a.) ***The cost of ingredients to make the item***. *Are they rare or valuable or plentiful and easy to get? Think of a diamond-difficult to get and not easily created. What are some other rare items that you can think of? Now, how about some plentiful items? Is there something in the U.S. that is cheaper or more expensive than in your country?*

        b.) ***The amount of time it takes to make the item***. *Is the item made by hand or machine?*

        c.) ***The Law of Supply and Demand***

Another important variable in price determination relates to the universal economic theory of Supply and Demand.

*"**Supply**"= the **quantity** of the product that you have available. In general, if you have a lot of something and you need to sell it you are going to charge less. Think of a huge crop of oranges. I need to sell them or they will go bad (rot).*

*"**Demand**"- How many consumers **want** the product. If a lot of people want more oranges, I might be able to raise my price, because people will be willing to pay more for something they want and they may be afraid I might run out.*

Let's look at an example of "Supply and Demand" for setting the price of a hotel room.

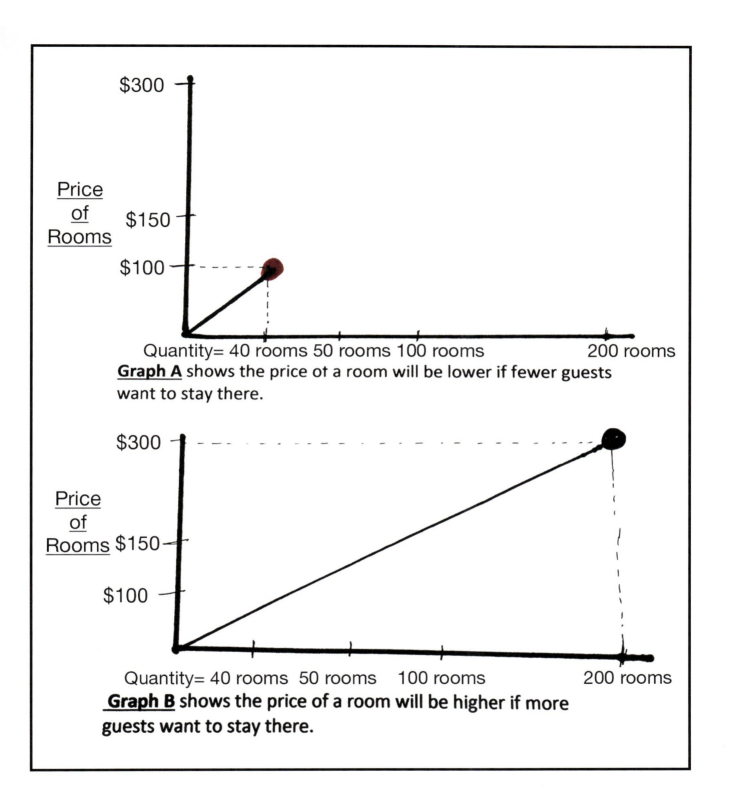

$300

Price
of
Rooms

$150

$100

Quantity= 40 rooms 50 rooms 100 rooms   200 rooms

Graph A shows the price ot a room will be lower if fewer guests want to stay there.

$300

Price
of
Rooms $150

$100

Quantity= 40 rooms 50 rooms   100 rooms   200 rooms

Graph B shows the price of a room will be higher if more guests want to stay there.

This is an example of a *Profit and Loss Statement.*

My Awesome Company

PROFIT AND LOSS

January - December 2018

	TOTAL
Income	$87,763.99
Cost of Goods Sold	$9,328.00
GROSS PROFIT	$78,435.99
Expenses	$5,707.06
NET OPERATING INCOME	$72,728.93
Other Income	$43.12
Other Expenses	$10,721.88
NET OTHER INCOME	$ -10,678.76
NET INCOME	$62,050.17

Economics Vocabulary

Income- the amount of money earned or also called earnings or profit.
Profit
Earnings

Cost of Goods Sold- the amount of money spent to produce the service or product

Gross profit- the amount of money made or earned **before** subtracting the expenses.

Expenses- the amount of money spent on paying employees (wages or payroll), shipping, gas and electric (utilities), etc.
Wages
Payroll
Utilities

Net Income- the amount of money earned **after** subtracting the expenses.
(Also called the **Bottom Line**)

Loss- negative amount of money on the **"Bottom Line."**

Unit 15
CUSTOMER SERVICE OPPORTUNITIES

Taking Food and Wine Orders

(The guest has been shown to their table and has been given the menu and wine list.)

Server- Welcome again to the _____. We are happy to have you. Would you like regular or bottled water?

Guest- We'd like regular water.

Server- Great. And may I get you started on a cocktail or a glass of wine before dinner or would you like wine with dinner?

Guest- I'd like a gin martini on the rocks and my wife will have a margarita straight up, no salt.

Server- Great. I'll bring those right away and give you a few more minutes to look at our menu. May I tell you tonight's specials?

Guest- Yes.

Server- Our chef has really been out-doing himself. We have a pan roasted halibut in a garlic-ginger sauce, stuffed veal breast, and filet mignon with a red wine sauce. I'll be right back with your drinks.

(The server returns with the drinks.)

Server- Have you decided what you would like? Do you have any questions about our menu?

Guest- What was that fish special again?

Server- Oh, that is a wonderful Alaskan Halibut with a garlic-ginger sauce. Very flavorful.

Guest- My wife will have that and I'll have the filet mignon.

Server- And how would you like that cooked?

Guest- I'd like my steak medium rare and my wife wants her fish not too well cooked— not dry.

Server- Oh, yes. Great choices. May I get you a starter?

Guest- No, I don't think so. But we would like some wine with dinner. What do you recommend?

Server- Well, since your wife is having the fish and you are having steak, how about this nice Merlot? That would pair nicely with both of your dishes.

Guest- Sounds great.

Server- Wonderful. I'll get all of that started.

(The server returns with the wine and serves it.)

Server- Enjoy your wine and I'll check on your orders.

(The server brings the entrees and pours more wine. The busser brings more bread and fills the water glasses.)

Server- Here is your halibut *(he places the fish in front of the guest)* and here is your filet. May I get you some freshly ground pepper?

Guest- Yes. And could I have some extra vegetables?

Server- Oh, yes. I am happy to get that for you.

(After serving the ground pepper and the extra vegetables, the server returns in a few minutes to ask........)

Server- How is everything tasting? Can I get you anything else?

Guest- Oh, everything is wonderful. Very delicious. Thank you.

Server- Oh, wonderful. I'll send your compliments to the chef.

(When guests appear to be finished.....)
Server- Are you finished?

Guests- Yes. That was delicious.

Server- May I get you coffee or may I tempt you with one of our homemade desserts?

Guest- Yes, let's look at the dessert menu.

(Server brings the dessert menu.)

Guest- My wife would like the crème brulee and I'll have the tiramisu.
And we'd both like coffee.

Server- Oh, those are my favorites! You won't be disappointed!

(Server brings the desserts. Guests are happy. When they are about finished with their coffee the server asks....)

Server- May I get you anything else? It has been our pleasure to have you. Shall I bring the check?

Guest- Yes. We thoroughly enjoyed our meal and your service was excellent. We'll be back.

Serving Wine

Would You Like Some Wine with Your Dinner?

Mr. and Mrs. Smith have just been seated and their server, Sally, is helping them with their order. They have ordered Caesar salads and two steaks.

Sally: May I offer you some wine with your dinner? Here is our wine list.

Mr. Smith: Yes. That would be nice. What would you recommend?

Sally: We have wines by the glass in this section and our bottles here.

Mr. Smith: Oh, I think we'd like a bottle, don't you, honey?

Mrs. Smith: Yes. That would be nice.

Sally: Well, since you are having steaks, we have some wonderful Cabernet Sauvignon. **(pronounced cabernay sauvinong).** The Beringer is very popular.

Mr. Smith: That sounds great.

Sally: Wonderful. I'll get that for you right away.

Sally returns to their table with the bottle of wine .

1. *She shows the label to Mr. Smith and repeats the name of the wine he ordered "* **This is the Beringer Cabernet. I know you'll like it.**
2. *Then she cuts the foil wrapper below the bulge on the neck of the bottle. She removes the foil wipes the top of the bottle.*
3. *After that, she pierces the cork with the spiral screw of the wine bottle opener.*
4. *Then she holds the bottle steady and turns the opener clockwise.*
5. *The levers of the opener lift as the screw goes into the cork.*
6. *When the spiral screw is almost at the bottom of the cork Sally presses down on the levers and pulls out the cork.*
7. *She unscrews the cork from the opener and puts it on the table near Mr. Smith.*
8. *She holds the bottle like she is shaking hands with it and with the label toward Mr. Smith she fills his glass with just an inch of wine. She gives the bottle a slight twist as she finishes pouring the wine.*
9. *Mr. Smith tastes the wine and says "This is fine."*
10. *Sally then serves Mrs. Smith, filling her glass to just half full. Then she fills Mr. Smith's glass to half full.*
11. *She puts the bottle on the table near Mr. Smith and says, "Enjoy your wine. I'll go check on your salads."*

Experience at a Casual Restaurant

It is a typical day at Comforts Deli and take-out restaurant. Let's listen.

ring, ring, ring..........

Silvia- Comforts. Silvia speaking. May I help you?

Customer- What time do you close today?

Slivia- I'm sorry. Could you repeat that, please?

Customer- What time do you close today?

Silvia- We close at 8pm.

Customer- What are your hours on Sundays?

Silvia- On Sundays we're open from 8am to 8pm.

Customer- OK, Thanks. (*customer hangs up*)

She takes an order for a chicken sandwich.

Silvia- How would you like your sandwich?
OR
What would you like on your sandwich?

Customer- I'd like mustard, mayo, lettuce, and pickles.

The next customer orders a slice of quiche.

Slivia- Would you like this warmed up?
OR
Would you like me to put this in the microwave for you?
OR
Would you like this heated up?